Positive Humanism

A Primer

I0449928

Written By

BO BENNETT, PHD

www.PositiveHumanism.com

Published by:

eBookIt.com
365 Boston Post Road, #311
Sudbury, MA 01776

Second edition - April 2015

publisher@ebookit.com
http://www.ebookit.com

Copyright 2015-2018, Archieboy Holdings, LLC
ISBN: 978-1-4566-2462-0

~~~~~

This book is dedicated to all our religious friends and family who may not agree with us, but care enough to try to understand us.

~~~~~

Table of Contents

Preface

Positive humanism is an applied secular humanistic philosophy based on the scientific findings of positive psychology that focuses on personal, professional, and societal flourishing. As an *applied* philosophy its focus is on ideas that lead to increased well-being. As a *secular humanistic* philosophy, there are no appeals to the supernatural, the magical, or the mystical. The philosophy is founded on reason and critical thinking. The philosophy is *science-based*, meaning it is void of the unsupported and/or exaggerated claims and the constant confusing of correlation with causality often found in the self-help genre. The philosophy is grounded in the theories of *positive psychology*, which is the study of the positive side of the mental health spectrum—*human flourishing*.

Positive humanism is not anti-religion; it is however anti-anti-humanism. There are many aspects of religions that are anti-humanism, such as denying gays' rights to marry, the belief that humanity is sinful and worthy of eternal punishment, the denial of science on religious grounds, and several others. However, it would be fallacious and unreasonable to be against an entire religion or worse, against religion itself, because of its anti-humanistic elements without considering its pro-humanistic elements, as well. There are many atheistic philosophies that take a hard approach by attacking religion and calling attention to its harmful elements. This approach has its purpose, but this is simply not what positive humanism is about. Positive humanism's focus is almost entirely on promoting positive humanism and defending it when necessary, but avoiding "attacking" religion (i.e., avoiding making aggressive arguments against religion). Abstaining from all arguments against all aspects of religious belief is not always possible, especially when such arguments are necessary to understand arguments for positive humanism. As a positive humanist, when I do make such arguments, I am committed to representing the religious argument as accurately as possible, and avoiding ridicule or other rhetorical devices that might otherwise reasonably offend.

Positive humanism is not for everyone. Having been a believer for the first 38 years of my life, and a non-believer going on five years now, I can say from personal experience that my overall well-being has increased significantly in that time. There are countless others with similar experiences who have celebrated their new life of reason. However, from a sociological and psychological perspective, it is clear that not everyone can benefit as I and others like me did from such a life change. For example, people from highly religious families or communities can be ostracized by intolerant family members and friends, lowering their well-being significantly.

My goal is to provide an evidence-based, secular philosophy of well-being for the rapidly growing number of people leaving religion and embracing reason, or just contemplating a more secular worldview, who want a higher quality of life than they had under their religious world view.

Positive humanism is not the same as positive psychology. In the simplest terms, there are parts of positive psychology that overlap with humanism. However, there are also parts of positive psychology that are not only outside of humanism, but also quite contrary to humanistic values. For example, Martin Seligman, considered the founder of positive psychology, stresses the importance of personal agency and responsibility. While this is certainly important, this focus greatly underestimates and undervalues the biological and social factors that influence behavior. Critics of positive psychology (of whom I am one) argue that this focus on personal agency leads to a "blame the victim" mentality. Essentially, it is the issue of free will—perhaps the most complex philosophical issue of the last couple millennia. Positive psychology also fails to "secularize" the well-being benefits that arise from religious and spiritual practices, and keeps them in a religious or spiritual context. This is understandable considering positive psychology is an American initiative, and an estimated 90% of Americans work within these contexts. Positive humanism translates these benefits to the secular.

Positive humanism is not the same as humanism. Positive humanism is different from humanism; however, unlike with positive psychology, there is nothing fundamentally at odds with humanism within positive humanism. Positive humanism takes the subset of humanism where the focus is on living a great life within a secular context. Positive humanism does not focus on *what is wrong* with religions, the supernatural, government, and society; it focuses on *what is right* with positive humanism. Let me be clear in saying that these more "negative" aspects of humanism are in no way unimportant or destructive; they are necessary to provide the foundation for positive humanism just like war is necessary to ensure the continued freedom of a (free) country.

The following sections are a collection of essays that provide the foundation for positive humanism and address some of the most frequently asked, yet rarely satisfactorily answered, questions about a secular philosophy. Whether you adopt this philosophy as your own, incorporate parts of it into an existing philosophy, or just gain a better understanding of one example of a secular worldview focused on good, this short read will be well worth your time.

POSITIVE HUMANISM: A PRIMER

Positive Humanism 2.0: Living the Good, Secular Life

The first known usage of the phrase "positive humanism" that resembles its modern usage can be found in a 1956 article, in the *Journal of Religion*, where the author was describing religious philosopher Albert Camus as a "non-Christian thinker" who is preoccupied with "questions of the nature and meaning of men, their hopes, their possibilities, and their destiny" (Hanna, 1956, p. 224). From 1956 to the late 70s, the phrase appeared sporadically in writing until in 1978 when Gerald A. Larue, published an essay simply titled, "Positive Humanism," in which he eloquently illustrated the joy, freedom, and meaning in life that he largely credits to his humanistic values. In June of 1989, Dr. Larue expanded his views on positive humanism and compiled them into a short book called *The Way of Positive Humanism*. Since then, there has been very little mention of positive humanism.

Much has changed since 1989.

My goal is to pick up where the late Dr. Larue left off by focusing on where the findings of the area of psychology known as *positive psychology* overlap with the values of humanism (see Figure 1).

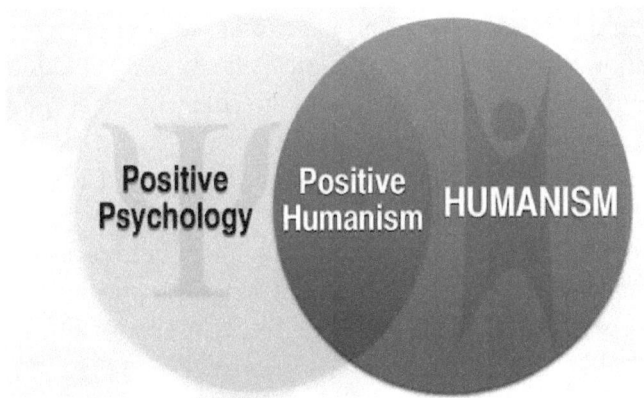

Figure 1. Venn Diagram

Why Positive Psychology?

In 1998, the then president of the American Psychological Association (APA), Martin Seligman, chose positive psychology as his theme, using the *humanistic psychology* of Abraham Maslow as the foundation. After a long career focusing on mental illness, Seligman realized that academic psychology was ignoring the other half of the mental health spectrum where we find well-being and human flourishing. Many self-help gurus have written about some aspect of human well-being (e.g., wealth, relationships, success, etc.) since early recorded history, and an explosion of the "self-help" genre was seen in the early 20th century. However, this genre has a questionable reputation at best given the countless unsupported and/or exaggerated claims made by the authors, the heavy use of anecdotal "evidence," the constant confusing of correlation with causality, and the annoyingly frequent references to the mystical and supernatural. Positive psychology uses the scientific method, based on *methodological naturalism* (i.e., no supernatural), to understand human well-being and flourishing. Similarly, a goal of humanism is to promote human well-being and flourishing without appealing to the supernatural. The union of the two seems almost "natural."

Why Positive Humanism?

In the past 15 years, researchers have found demonstrable ways to help individuals live better lives, most recently measured by human *flourishing,* or experiencing a high level of well-being. Flourishing is defined as living "within an optimal range of human functioning, one that connotes goodness, generativity, growth, and resilience" (Fredrickson & Losada, 2005, p. 678). A recent large-scale study measured the flourishing of over 43,000 Europeans in 23 countries. Denmark, consistently ranked as one of the least religious countries in the world, ranked the highest with 41% of its citizens surveyed qualified as flourishing (Huppert & So, 2013). While no causality is implied, this indicates that positive psychology and humanism are certainly compatible. But humanism also extends beyond one's own well-being. Positive humanism recognizes that one of the best ways of achieving a higher level of well-being is by helping others through concrete, prosocial acts (Rudd, Aaker, & Norton, 2014). Through a combination of humanistic, evidence-based self-improvement and prosocial efforts, positive humanism lives up to the aspirations of humanism.

I can think of no better, worthwhile goal in life than contributing to human well-being and flourishing. While I am confident that fellow humanists will embrace positive humanism, I can only hope that these ideas will also resonate with our theistic brothers and sisters who believe that priority should be given to serving a deity, even at the expense of humanity. For this to happen, I believe that we need to lead by example. When others are amazed by our passion for life and our contribution to humanity, it will be a testament to the efficacy and practicality of the philosophy known as *positive humanism*.

The Morality of Positive Humanism

One time, I remember, going into the Strand, a poor and infirm old man craved his alms. He beholding him with eyes of pity and compassion, put his hands in his pocket, and gave him 6d. Said a divine (that is Dr. Jasper Mayne) that stood by— 'Would you have done this, if it had not been Christ's command?' 'Yes,' said he. 'Why?' said the other. 'Because,' said he, 'I was in pain to consider the miserable condition of the old man; and now my alms, giving him some relief, doth also ease me.'

- **John Aubrey**, Brief Lives (late 17th Century) on Thomas Hobbes

Understandably, theists find comfort in the idea that there exists a God who is the foundation of human morality. A common theistic understanding is that good and evil are not dependent on God nor superordinate to God, but rather that good is God's *nature*. This provides theists with the idea of an *objective* morality that is absolute and unchanging—one that also happens to be knowable by mankind. However, this belief often comes at the expense of collective well-being. Aside from the strong probability of God not existing, there are also many serious flaws with the classic theistic position of God as the foundation of morality that are beyond the scope of positive humanism. This chapter is about how humanists can understand morality in a world without God, and explain it to others.

So Man Created God in His Own Image

From a psychological perspective, God can be defined as humanity's projection of human ideals and values. This explains why "God's" position on gay rights, forbidden foods, sexual practices, capital punishment, forgiveness and justice, getting into Heaven, avoiding Hell, and virtually every other political, moral, and imagined issue is a clear reflection of the culture and the believer, and not the other way around. It is easy to imagine a single God with one morality, but if morality is based on human ideals and values, it would reason that it would naturally contain variation given the seven billion humans that comprise what we call "human ideals." This variation is responsible for the subjectivity and relativity of morality that many people fear.

Objectivity, Relativity, or Both?

The thought of living in a world where what is "right" and "good" is decided by people and not some transcendent law is terrifying to most—even those who don't believe in any gods. The idea that there is an *objective morality*, that is, a universal law that exists that makes something right or wrong, good or bad, for everyone, in all situations, at all times, is a comforting thought and generally harmless. However, it is the belief that we have direct knowledge of this objective morality that is dangerous and a major cause of conflict on both personal and global levels. While we may never know if such "moral truths" exist independently of the human mind, there are ways of understanding morality that are internally consistent (i.e., philosophically sound), in line with scientific understanding, have both personal and prosocial benefits, and do not rely on magical thinking or the supernatural. The first step is to recognize that the "objective" and "subjective/relative" dichotomy in morality is a false one. Morality can have components of both, addressing the fears of the "anything would be permissible" crowd while not requiring some unexplainable magic law.

The Collective Well-Being of Humanity: The Humanistic Moral Foundation

As demonstrated by the opening quote, *empathy* is the biological foundation of what constitutes much of moral action. But this feeling-based foundation can only get us so far, especially in a world where physical distance and rational facts replace the intimate and emotionally charged climate of our ancestors. As humanists, we have *chosen* to ground morality in human well-being just like theists have *chosen* to ground their morality in their specific god or holy book. As humanists, however, we should acknowledge this as a choice rather than some universal or divine law. In one sense, this is an objective morality because it is based on the well-being of *every* human, and what is "good" and "right" is *always* based on human well-being. In another sense, well-being is ultimately a *subjective* concept, meaning that the specific feelings, thoughts, and behaviors that constitute well-being are not the same for everyone. For example, my personal sense of well-being is largely dependent on the achievement domain whereas yours may rely mostly on positive emotion. Therefore, you may feel it is immoral for me to ask employees to work overtime to complete a major project, whereas I may see it as immoral not to. Objectively, one of the two actions will lead to greater collective well-being despite our subjective beliefs and values—*we just can't know which*.

Morality is unimaginably complex primarily because of our inability to predict long-term outcomes and far-reaching effects of our actions. In other words, we cannot always predict how an action, behavior, or thought might affect the overall well-being of humanity. In the previous example, we don't know which course of action will ultimately lead to greater collective well-being so we must act according to the best available evidence and be quick to correct and learn from our mistakes. People on all sides of issues frequently believe they have the moral high ground because they believe they can better predict effects on well-being than their opponents. No matter what people believe about well-being, there is some objective level of subjective well-being that is experienced even though we most likely will never be able to measure it with 100% accuracy.

No Moral Anarchy Nor Utility

As long as morality is grounded in human well-being, "anything" is *not* permissible. Rape is wrong because it clearly subtracts from human well-being. The pleasure the rapist might feel from the act pales in comparison to the suffering of the victim, the victim's family, the victim's community, and the world at large might experience by living in a world where something like that can happen to them or someone about whom they care. In this example, we see that collective well-being extends beyond utility and the direct benefits of a few, and incorporates the *psychological well-being* of all humanity. It is not morally permissible for doctors to grab a healthy person from the waiting room and dissect him for his organs in order to save ten lives. The idea of living in a world where such an act is permissible (and can happen to you or your loved ones) does far more damage to overall well-being than saving ten lives.

Changing Morality: A Tough Pill To Swallow

Even though there is an objectively correct moral choice (albeit often unknowable), the collective well-being on which morality is based is subject to change over time. An individual or group of people can have an effect on morality if they can influence others' thoughts, feelings, and beliefs on well-being. For example, if society generally accepts that gay marriage is immoral, the *idea* of gay marriage may have negative psychological effects (no matter how irrational it may seem to us) on the vast majority of people that result in decreased overall well-being. If a person or group can influence enough people to change their thoughts, feelings, and beliefs, then the balance of negative to positive well-being can shift to the point where the moral position changes. This idea is difficult to accept for some because of the *historian's fallacy,* an error in reasoning that occurs when one assumes that decision makers of the past viewed events from the same perspective and having the same information as those subsequently analyzing the decision. It may be incomprehensible for us today to imagine how an issue such as women's voting rights could have ever even been an issue worthy of debate, but this is because we are putting a moral issue of 100 years ago in today's moral climate.

Morality does change over time, but only because our thoughts, feelings, and beliefs about the world are constantly changing based on new information being available. Understood in this way, *the relativity of morality is temporal only—objective in the moment, but relative over time.* Morality is not geographically relative since the foundation of morality, human well-being, is geographically ubiquitous. A tribe living in the jungle that eats their babies as a form of population control may experience a high level of well-being within their tribe, but knowledge of such a practice by the rest of humanity has a deleterious effect on overall well-being. From a humanist perspective, the well-being of humanity takes precedence over cultural practices that violate human rights even if these practices might be "free expressions of religion." In the humanist world view, there is no privileged status for religious practices that negatively affect human well-being making them exempt from moral judgment.

A Complex Topic Too Often Made Simplistic

I have presented examples that generally do not present moral dilemmas—issues such as rape, infanticide, and cannibalism. As we have seen, despite any objectivity that may exist in a morality grounded in well-being, our inherent inability to know the long term and far reaching effects that an action might have on well-being adds the subjective element to morality, and the reason for moral disagreement. Like it or not, morality is *functionally democratic*. What is considered moral is a collective reflection of human ideals and values. It may be the case that our collective moral judgment is one that detracts from our well-being but we just don't know it, or it may be that the moral majority is in need of an attitude change due to the suffering of an ignored or unknown minority. If there is a "moral truth" we should accept, it is that morality is a highly complex issue that cannot be encapsulated in one rule or even ten commandments.

As humanists, we must not accept "moral truths" (including mine) without carefully considering the effects they may have on the well-being of all of humanity. Science can certainly *inform* moral decisions since, although far from perfect, well-being is a measurable construct. We must practice empathy and anticipate how choices might affect the well-being of others. We need to think both short-term and long-term. Most importantly, we must have the wisdom and the courage to distinguish morality from obedience, and act in accordance with maximizing collective well-being to the best of our ability.

Religion: A Middleman to Well-Being

It seems as if a new study is released almost daily showing another benefit of religious belief. As a humanist, these articles used to detract from my positive emotion dimension of well-being because theists would often use this research to attempt to justify their supernatural beliefs. However, as a social scientist, I could not just fall victim to the confirmation bias and ignore the studies that might weaken my humanist position by providing more reasons to adopt a religious world view. With a change in attitude, these articles became an opportunity for understanding. I began to understand that religion turns out to be like an unnecessary middleman hawking products that you can buy direct. Instead of costing you extra money, it costs you a piece of your intellectual integrity, and in some cases, much more. In other words, *religion is a means to an end*. That end, I will argue, is well-being.

Many middlemen do add value. They wouldn't survive very long in an open market unless they did. Religion adds value. It is a category consisting of countless prepackaged beliefs that have some form of continuity and internal consistency (i.e., beliefs that are generally consistent with each other, not necessarily with the scientific method, observation, or even reality). This packaged belief system is very attractive to many people, especially those who are much less tolerant of uncertainty and ambiguity than others (Hogg, Adelman,

& Blagg, 2010), are more prone to magical thinking (Caldwell-Harris, Wilson, LoTempio, & Beit-Hallahmi, 2011), and/or are unaware of other philosophies that focus on prosocial values. But like with most middlemen, with a little knowledge and a tad of effort, we can bypass them and get a better deal. *Positive humanism is that better deal.*

A Means to an End

When we say we want money, it is extremely unlikely that we want germ-covered paper with pictures of deceased notables on them. We don't even want the things the money can buy, such as a new pair of shoes. What we ultimately want is our lives to be better in some way. *Well-being theory* (Seligman, 2012) and its five dimensions (positive emotion, engagement, relationships, achievement, and meaning/purpose or PERMA) is the one of the best ways we can define in a useful way (i.e., operationalize) what it means to live a better life. The new pair of shoes might increase our positive emotion by buying them, showing them off, and receiving compliments on them. Perhaps we also believe that the new shoes will help increase our chances of finding a romantic partner (relationships). Increasing these two dimensions lead to an overall increase in our well-being. This is one of the key understandings in positive psychology—*that our wants and desires can be reduced to aspects of well-being.*

When a study names religion as a factor that increases well-being, "religion" is used as a generic term that packages many factors that lead to well-being. A critical look at any of these factors reveals that each factor in itself is a means, not an end. For example, it is well understood now that one of religion's greatest benefits is the sense of belonging (e.g., Seul, 1999), often realized by community church attendance. This is part of the relationship dimension of well-being. Of course, this sense of belonging can be met in other ways that have nothing to do with religion.

"Proof" That Religion is Just a Middleman

Religiosity and spirituality, in many cases (certainly not all) are contributing factors to well-being, although you will notice that neither is one of the five dimensions of well-being. In psychology, "dimensions" of a construct such as well-being are not chosen *ad hoc* or selected based on a cute acronym (although PERMA is pretty cute). There is a scientific process called *factor analysis* that is used to identify as few necessary dimensions as possible while eliminating the unnecessary ones. The reason religion, spirituality, or "God" did not make the cut is because aspects of all these are subsumed under one or more of the five dimensions of PERMA. In a way, this is scientific evidence that neither religiosity nor spirituality is a significant part of well-being.

Positive humanism explores the many alternatives to religious belief that lead to well-being. There is no need for "faith" (i.e., believing in something disproportionate to the evidence), no need to accept beliefs that contradict with our current scientific understanding, and there is no authority figure or authoritative texts to follow. If your goal in life is well-being, than even positive humanism is just a means to an end—it's just the more direct route, and an awesome ride!

Making Sense of Reason

How can one *account for* and *justify* the use of reason within a secular framework? Some might suggest that this question is meaningless. For example, the "What happened before the beginning of time?" question is meaningless because "before" is an indicator of a point in time (temporal). So without time, "before" has no meaning in that context and makes the question meaningless. Just as "before" can only be understood within the context of time, "account for" and "justify" can only be understood within the context of reason. Others might suggest that to justify something requires reason; therefore, we are using reason to justify itself. This can either be viewed as something that is *self-evident* or as a fallacy of *circular reasoning*—largely depending on one's existing world view. Here philosophy demonstrates to be a more useful tool to the biased philosopher rather than to the truth seeker. It is important to note that meaninglessness, self-evidence, and circularity are possible philosophical answers to what is an ultimately a poorly worded question. What we want is a scientific answer to the real question: *What is the origin of reason and can we trust it?*

The Origin of Reason

Reason is not a "thing" that exists outside somewhere in (or outside) the universe; it is an ability dependent upon a brain capable of such a process. It is clearly an evolved ability, fueled by emotion and favored by natural selection. The higher-order neural processing of humanity, today, was far less developed in our ancient ancestors and non-existent in our ancestors if you go back far enough (Richards, 1989). Neuroscience pinpoints the areas of the brain where these higher order processes (i.e., reasoning; Pinker, 1999) primarily take place, and by studying the brains of primates, other mammals, and more primitive life forms, we find demonstrable evidence for the evolution of reason.

The Foundation of Reason

Our primal brain functions are based on emotion, and this emotionally-based functioning continues today to be a significant part of our brain function (Pinker, 1999). As biological organisms, we are compelled to a state of homeostasis. Negative feelings cause us to take actions to mitigate those feelings. Conversely, we are compelled to actions and behaviors that result in positive feelings. But we are creatures of both emotion and reason, and it is this emotional neural processing that serves as the foundation for our reason by *associating outcomes of the reasoning process with feeling-based (affective) states*. For example, our raw, primal emotions may tell us to grab that delicious looking piece of cake from that woman's hand and eat it (the cake, not the woman's hand) because it would taste good (again, the cake and not the hand). Thanks to our ability to foresee possible future consequences of our actions and behaviors, our reason tells us that taking the cake would result in us ending up in the red on the balance sheet of positive feelings, that is, having the cake (and eating it, too) would result in a predictably lower level of well-being.

The Development of Reason in Our Species

According to the theory of natural selection, mutations can either be adaptive or maladaptive. These mutations result in the different genetic makeup of a cell (*genotypes*) which result in different observable traits or characteristics of the organism (*phenotypes*). The ability of our ancestors to reason better did not happen by magic or by "chance" (selection is the opposite of chance); *it is a product of natural selection.* Imagine early hominids just starting to use higher-order processing. Those who use reason effectively manage to stay alive and pass on their genes at a higher rate than those who could not reason. Today, we are the result of countless ancestors who out reasoned the competition or at the very least, were not out reasoned by the competition to the point of not having or seizing the opportunity to procreate. It is clear that reason is an evolutionarily adaptive function.

The Secular Justification for Reason

While we can look to evolution and natural selection as having hundreds of thousands of years of evidence justifying our general use of reason, we can better justify our use and the high value we put on reason simply because *it works*. That is, the repeated use of good reasoning leads to outcomes that increase our well-being. Ironically, or perhaps paradoxically, giving a reason to justify our use of reason seems wrong. No matter what reason we give (even"God did it"), it is still a reason. While there may be no escape from this, we can justify our use of reason not through reasoning but through our actions. Living a life based on reason leads to greater well-being, and that should be good enough for any humanist.

Exploring the "F" Word: Freewill

For over 2500 years, humans have been debating the issue of freewill. There are numerous books on the topic, entire university courses, countless recorded lectures on the Internet, and even more unique thoughts and opinions on freewill. I promise you, this will not be another opinionated rant claiming to have solved the 2500 year-old mystery, nor will it be a lecture rehashing the arguments made by dead white men, nor will it be an essay comprising philosophically pompous terms such as "compatibilism", "libertarianism," and "contra-causal." What this will be is *a* solution (not *the* solution) to the philosophical problem of freewill from a positive humanist's perspective.

Whether you realized it or not, the problem of freewill pervades virtually every aspect of our lives from social justice to personal success and ignoring it or just assuming we have it are not good options. Another option that we have is to spend an eternity (or at least a very long time) looking for "the" answer, while living with an inconsistent view of freewill that leads to unnecessary human suffering and a lack of prosperity. This, too, is not a good option. Yet another option, consistent with the scientific approach, is to choose the best answer that is consistent with our observations and the natural world, one that doesn't require special pleading or supernatural intervention, and one that empowers us while promoting kindness and helping us to realize that hatred, revenge, and contempt are irrational emotions not worthy of expression by a being capable of reason. This is a good option.

What is "Freewill?"

There are literally dozens, perhaps hundreds of different definitions of freewill. The reason for this, I suspect, is partly due to the fact that the concept of freewill is nebulous and partly due to the fact that our language lacks the terminology to define freewill accurately. For the purpose of this article and within the context of positive humanism, a basic and general understanding of the term from virtually any perspective is all that is required. We can define freewill as simply *the possibility to have made a different choice than the choice that was made*.

The Real Problem of Freewill

If you wanted to, could you become a Nobel laureate? A billionaire? How about a teacher? A firefighter? A McDonald's employee working the drive-through window? Clearly some paths are more difficult than others, but are they all *possible*? If the motivational gurus are right, we can do *anything* if we "put our minds to it." We are in charge of our destiny. The only thing holding us back, is us. But what if we don't *want* to become any of these things? Many discussions of freewill overlook this simple fact: freewill is not just about doing what you want; it is about *metadesires*, or wanting what we want, wanting what we want to want, and so on. For example, I don't want to be a McDonald's employee working the drive-through window. Frankly, and perhaps it's my hubris, but I feel that I am overqualified for that position, and it would not be fulfilling for me. I believe that I could hold this position if I wanted to, I just don't want to. But can I make myself want to? I believe if I made myself want to, I could want to, but I don't want to make myself want to. Could I make myself want to make myself want to? You get the point. The real question is, what is behind these desires that guide our thoughts, actions, and behaviors, and are we in control of that? My response to this ultimate question is, *it doesn't matter*.

The Freewill Controversy

Although I believe in a world of cause and effect with the possibility of randomness and uncaused causes, I also accept the empirical fact of decades of psychological research that demonstrates convincingly that our beliefs and desires are part of this causal chain of events. So far there is nothing too controversial here. The freewill controversy begins when claims are made whether these beliefs and desires that are part of the causal chain of events in the world originate from *outside the causal chain or within it*. Again, from a positive humanism perspective, *it doesn't matter*.

What Does Matter

While science may never uncover the mystery behind the concept of freewill, it has provided us with ample empirical evidence showing that there are different degrees of freedom; external factors have a powerful influence on our thoughts, actions, and behaviors; and belief is strongly correlated with action and behaviors. These three ideas are of utmost importance when it comes to morality, politics, and virtually all of our social interactions.

Different degrees of freedom. Both a smoker and a non-smoker can choose to not pick up a cigarette, although what some might consider the "freedom" of the smoker is curtailed by the strong biological drives and psychological processes known as addiction. The smoker might claim that he or she could quit if he or she wanted to, but it is these environmental and biological factors that at least contribute to the desire to smoke, overpowering the desire to quit. These biological drives and psychological processes are not separate from the smoker; they are part of who the person is. Once we dispel this notion that the self is a magical soul or some kind of ghost in the machine, separate from our biology and environment, we realize how much we are connected to this earth and the people around us. Understanding that some people have more choices than others allows us to be more empathetic and understanding rather than judgmental.

External influences. While those who reject the idea of freewill generally claim that all of our thoughts, behaviors, and actions are a result of environment and biology, proponents of freewill generally claim that there is "something else" that allows us to choose independently from the determinism of our environment and biology. The "something else" is often a supernatural "something else," making it unknowable to the methodological naturalism that governs the scientific method. In other words, if there is "something else," science cannot (by definition) ever find it. Rather than speculate or believe on "faith" that this "something else" exists, we can form our belief based on what we do know—what science can tell us, which is, unequivocally, that our thoughts, behaviors, and actions are greatly influenced by forces and factors outside our control such as genetics, chemistry, social influence (e.g., persuasion and manipulation), biological drives (e.g., thirst, hunger, sex), education, and so much more. Again, our choices are not made in a vacuum. Using reason requires drawing upon the information available to us, and all of us have a different set of information as a result of our unique histories of which proportionally, we had very little control if any.

Belief, action, and behavior. While within the realm of science we must be very careful about making causal claims, we can say that belief is strongly correlated with actions and behaviors. Philosophically we can posit that human belief is a part of the causal chain of events that unfold in the universe. Action begins with belief, and without belief, action is less likely to be taken. The beliefs we hold to be true about ourselves are the basis for our behavior—how we treat others and how we treat ourselves. *Deep philosophical musings about if we really are free to make any changes in our lives affect our beliefs in our self-efficacy and have a real, measurable effect, on our actions and behaviors.* We can say that we need to have more "faith" in ourselves and humanity, but I would argue that faith, even in this context, is unnecessary given the abundant body of scientific research we have supporting the fact that where we find stronger belief, we find measurable manifestations of that belief. The motivational gurus do appear to be on the right track with this one.

Freewill and the Positive Humanist

On the one hand, the scientific approach to the freewill issue allows us to have greater empathy for those who find themselves in less-than-ideal circumstances rather than take a "blame the victim" approach. On the other hand, we realize that *we* are external influences on others. *We are agents of change.* We can introduce new information into the lives of others that lead them to change their beliefs and behaviors. However, we are up against a lifetime of environmental and biological influences, and neither we nor the people we try to change are to blame for any lack of effectiveness. As for eliciting change in our own

27

behavior, we can seek out people who can help us, even if just through motivation, encouragement, or social support.

We must work to find more effective ways to be agents of change while realizing that sometimes our best efforts might not be good enough, but until we honestly give our best effort, we will never really know.

"Balance" Does Not Have To Mean Being Irrational

Why would anyone be anti-rationality, anti-critical thinking, or anti-reason? The answer has to do with people's misunderstandings of what these terms mean, and more to the point, what they do not mean. This problem could best be understood by thinking of the highly logical but emotionally void "Spock" character in *Star Trek*. I have heard too many people justify superstitious, irrational, and faith-based beliefs as a way to "balance" their humanity by experiencing life on a more emotional or "spiritual" level. These people are half right, and half wrong. They are right in that a life devoid of emotion, imagination, and passion is not much of a life at all. They are wrong in believing that these experiences require the suspension of rationality, the need to embrace the supernatural, or the need to believe something disproportionate to the evidence.

Kicking Old Ladies

I can best explain why this "balance" hypothesis is a bad one through an analogy. It is safe to say that most people would agree that morality is a good thing, that is doing what is right and good over what is wrong and bad. We would not claim that we should "balance" our morality with *immorality*. In order to embrace our humanity, we don't need to kick an old lady every week and rob a bank once a year. We strive to live moral lives and any deviation from that path is considered a wrong turn. But what about brushing our teeth, going for a walk, listening to music, or the countless other actions that are not considered "moral?" To claim that because an action is not moral, then it must be immoral, is not only wrong, but fallacious reasoning (i.e., a *false dichotomy*). Actions can also be *amoral*, which means there is no moral value associated with the action. When we scratch our head, sneeze, or do push-ups, we are not acting immorally, we are simply engaging in amoral actions. *We are not required to behave immorally when our behavior does not require morality.*

Arationality: Neither Rational Nor Irrational

Awe, elation, and love are some of the most meaningful human experiences that are not results of reason, rationality, or critical thinking. However, this does not mean they are the result of being unreasonable, irrational, or using poor thinking. These are what philosopher Rosalind Hursthouse refers to as *arational* processes (Hursthouse, 1991), or experiences that are not subject to rational scrutiny. This confusion leads to problems that arise when *an arational experience is confused with an irrational belief based on that experience.*

Love and "Soulmates"

Love is arguably one of the most wonderful of all human experiences. When we experience love, we feel a warm sensation all throughout our bodies. This is an arational process. A common irrational belief associated with love is the belief that we found our one and only "soulmate" on a planet of 7 billion people (a statistical impossibility). This is also a potentially devastating belief to future happiness in the statistically likely case the marriage fails. This irrational "soulmate" belief is not required to experience love.

A Feeling Is Not the Same as an Explanation of the Feeling

Awe is another of the great human experiences. Looking down on the world from 10,000 feet or out into the universe on a clear and starry night can certainly lead to what many would call a "spiritual" experience, or the feeling of being just a tiny part of something much greater than oneself. However, many take this experience and create or adopt a narrative in an attempt to explain the feeling (e.g., God). This is the forming of an unnecessary and irrational belief based on the arational experience. Believing you know something you can't is not required to experience awe, in fact, this only robs people of more experiences—wonder and human curiosity.

Keep the Good, Lose the Bad

There is an added benefit to embracing the rational. We can limit and control the effects of negative arational processes such as anger, jealousy, grief, shame, fear, and even hatred. For example, hatred is the result of a strong emotional response. If we think critically by seeing the situation from the perspective of the target of our hate, we start to replace the hatred with understanding which reduces or can even eliminate the negative emotional response, while enhancing the quality of our lives through better relationships.

We do not need irrationality any more than we need immorality. Rejecting the irrational and unreasonable in no way limits the human experience; it enhances it. Through arational processes, we can experience the full range of human emotions and use our rationality to form the most accurate and rationally-based beliefs. We can use our critical thinking skills to mitigate the damage done by negative emotional responses. Being a rational and reasonable critical thinker does not mean being an emotionally bankrupt shell of a human. We embrace the arational such as elation, affection, awe, wonder, and love for what they are—human experiences that make life worth celebrating.

On Dying and Living

Let's face it, the thought of dying is quite unpleasant—*and this is a very good thing*. This means that our will to live is strong and our actions, both conscious and unconscious, will be in line with this desire, protecting us from harm and being conducive toward achieving longevity. Evolution has all but ensured that we maintain a strong will to live and avoid death, which includes maintaining a healthy aversion to death. Those of our ancestors who welcomed death with open arms, at least from an early age, would have won themselves a *Darwin award* and all but eliminated themselves from the gene pool. Our ancestors are those who balanced a healthy respect for death with an appreciation for life. To increase our well-being, we don't need to believe in a perfect afterlife, and we don't need to lie to ourselves and others by pretending that we like the idea that we will almost certainly one day cease to exist. If we want to increase our wealth, we might cut back on expenses while increasing our income. Likewise, if we want to increase our well-being, we can minimize the negatives associated with dying while maximizing the positives associated with living.

How Did You Feel About Not Being Born Yet?

Of course, this question is meant to be ironic because if we are not born, we don't exist, so we can't feel (did I really have to explain that?). But the question is also meant to make one realize that the thought of non-existence is only something those who exist can experience. That is, once we are dead, we are not going to be concerned about anything. The problem is it's the present "us" that frets about our future non-existence, but why exactly? I will argue that "fretting" can be used to motivate us to live a better life.

Why Do We Fear Death?

As mentioned earlier, from an evolutionary perspective, our fear of death is deeply ingrained, just like other biological drives. But there are also unique reasons why each of us may fear death. For example, one might worry about how his or her death would affect his or her family. Once the fears have been identified, we can address them from a humanist perspective.

Facing Reality (a Humanist Perspective)

Those who believe in an eternal paradise where we are all reunited with our loved ones, embrace what is referred to as a *positive delusion*, or a belief held firm contrary to available evidence, in which the belief has positive effects. Much research has demonstrated that a belief in the afterlife does contribute to happiness and well-being (e.g., Smith, Range, & Ulmer, 1991), but these studies do not measure the related decrease in well-being resulting from the effects of holding these kinds of beliefs. For example, a widow may believe that she will be reunited with her husband in Heaven, and therefore spend the rest of her life pushing away other potential partners, which can have a serious deleterious effect on well-being. This focus on "the next life" comes at a clear expense in this life. As humanists, our focus is on the overall well-being in this life, *and only this life*. We might be tempted to conclude that one's belief in Heaven is not authentic, since he or she avoids death just like the rest of us. Rationally speaking, if one was certain Heaven existed why would anyone hang around this place? The answer has to do with something I call *holistic dissonance*—a cognition in conflict with non-cognitive desires or biological drives. A good analogy is one's strong biological desire to eat way too much junk food despite the rational understanding that a large amount of junk food has negative effects on one's health. Our behaviors are strongly influenced by evolutionary pressures, and this influence can be extremely difficult to overcome. In the case of believing in Heaven, evolution is protecting us from our own possibly fatal behaviors resulting from unsupported beliefs.

Taking Action

The fear that one's death will have a serious negative impact on one's family's well-being is a justified one, but not one that can't be overcome by taking the necessary precautions to ensure one's family is well taken care of, which includes not only financially, but emotionally. Perhaps one might make

35

sure his last will and testament is updated, his businesses can survive and continue to make money for his family, he talks with his wife and makes sure she understands that he has no problem with her remarrying (after he is gone, of course) if that is her desire, and he become the best father to his children *now* rather than "someday" when everything is perfect and he "has more time" for them. These specific actions would increase one's well-being by lessening the negative emotions associated with the worry of death and increasing the quality of relationships.

We cannot claim certainty about the impossibility of some form of positive existence post death—a fact where even the most rational humanist may find a ray of hope. But we don't live our lives based on remote possibilities, rather we live our lives based on realistic probabilities. The best we can do is be prepared for death and mitigate the associated worries and fears, then spend the rest of our lives focusing not on death, but life.

This is not a practice; this is the big game. This is not a rehearsal; this is both opening night and the final performance. This is not some test; this is real life. So put your game face on and enjoy the ride!

About Me (the Author)

Positive humanism represents everything about which I am passionate, even though the ideas outlined in this book are the product of frustration. Once you read why, I am confident you will empathize with my frustrations, and understand why I feel that promoting positive humanism is the most worthy of all social causes.

I was raised Catholic by parents who were more cultural Catholics than practicing Catholics, though I was sent to Sunday school and received the childhood sacraments. After being "confirmed" in the 8th grade, I was done with practicing religion, although I did not yet question my belief in God that was instilled in me by my parents and Christian culture, and when asked, I referred to myself as a "Christian," thinking, at the time, that the only choices were either "Christian" or "Jew." One could say, using modern terms, that this is when I became a "none."

I come from what most would consider a very dysfunctional family. While I will skip the depressing details, let me just say that I loved my parents very much and I am sure they loved me. The dysfunction was mostly between my parents and their lifelong battles with their own personal "demons" (say what you will about religion, they have some wonderful metaphors). Despite these less than ideal conditions, I remained generally a positive kid and stayed away from drugs and alcohol (I remain dry to this day); however, I did need an escape.

My Drug of Choice: Tony Robbins

As a temporary escape from my reality, I would listen to my sister's and mom's self-help cassette tapes, which included the philosophical and pseudoscientific ramblings of the greats such as Denis Waitley, Zig Ziglar, Tony Robbins, and many others. I come from a family of entrepreneurs. My sister was in real-estate at the time, my mom was in sales, my father was an inventor, and my brother had a screen printing business.

My drive and passion for being an entrepreneur was always strong and apparently has a strong genetic component, so it is difficult to know how much of a part my obsession with self-help played in my future financial successes. However, one cannot underestimate the power of motivation, encouragement, and in some cases, inspiration (no matter how misguided). And I cannot dismiss the positive emotions frequently experienced when listening to these programs and visualizing my own future, even though these programs were more often based on science-fiction than science.

Jackpot!

In 1995, after I graduated with my Bachelor's degree in Marketing from Bryant University, I started a little web hosting business at a time when only a few percent of businesses knew what web hosting was. This little business grew to a major business that I sold to a publicly traded company in 2001 for 20 million dollars. As the years passed, I would start and sell several businesses ranging from small websites to 18,000 square foot data centers. I spent some serious time reflecting on my success and how I could help others succeed. I devoted a full year to writing *Year To Success*, a book Donald Trump called, "an inspiration to anyone who reads it." The main premise of the book is at the heart of my philosophy and one of the "truths" in life that many people seem to miss. Success is not a result of a few steps or "secrets," but hundreds or perhaps even thousands of contributing factors, many over which we have varying levels of control. It would be several years later when I would realize that this contributing factor idea also applies to virtually every learned skill, talent, and psychological construct, including happiness and well-being. A fact that psychology has established long ago.

The Frustration Begins

The process of writing *Year To Success* ignited something new in me—*critical thinking, reason, and skepticism.* In doing the research for my book I have reread over 100 self-help books and programs, and realized how "inaccurate," to put it politely, most of them were. This genre has a questionable reputation at best for a reason—the countless unsupported and/or exaggerated claims made by the authors, the heavy use of anecdotal "evidence," the constant confusing of correlation with causality, and the annoyingly frequent references to the mystical and supernatural. My book, while better than most, was still guilty of some of these "self-help crimes" (I am happy to say that the latest revised edition is now crime free).

Over the next several years, my passion for critical thinking and skepticism continued to grow, and this internal conflict between my two alter-egos: the reality seeking skeptic and the positive success guru, reached a point where I could no longer, in good conscience, agree to do speaking events about achieving success. Still with an unbridled passion for speaking, I started a skeptical podcast that exposed the dishonesty common in marketing, and I created a presentation debunking the many myths of success. But this was just the beginning. Being financially secure, I devoted full time to exploring religions, specifically Christianity—extending my skepticism beyond self-help. It didn't take long before I was an admitted atheist (reading the entire Bible tends to do that to a person). I realized that beliefs about both religion and success are ultimately psychological phenomena, and could best be explained through understanding psychology. It was this realization that prompted me to go back to school, get my master's degree in general psychology, and a PhD in social psychology.

Becoming an Angry Atheist, Then a Positive Humanist

While I was exploring religion, I started a website where I collected 1000s of hours of debates as a way to help others who were going through the same "journey of truth" as I was. I created a discussion group on the site, as well, where I would devote several hours per day (for over 3 years) defending reason. Not just from the claims of religion, but all sorts of pseudoscience including astrology, homeopathy, talking with the dead, astral projection, ESP, levitation—you name it. Most of the debates got ugly, and I realized that I was becoming a person I did not want to be. I grew tired of telling people what they should *not* believe. I also grew tired of theists' claims that life does not "make sense" or is

41

"pointless" without God. Claims that atheists are immoral and untrustworthy. Claims that atheists could not experience awe and wonder. Religion does provide structure for many people by combining countless unknowns in life into a single unknown (i.e., "the mystery of God"), and my atheistic position was simply a disbelief in any gods, which is not a philosophy nor a useful world view. I eventually shut down the discussion group and made a conscious effort to leave the role as the "angry atheist" while going back to the person that I really liked to be—the person who focused on helping people succeed. This time; however, I would do so using the scientific foundation of positive psychology and humanistic world view. This means I would approach the topic as an academic rather than a guru, focus on the scientifically established multidimensional construct of well-being rather than the nebulous and illusive idea of "success," and stress the importance of prosocial acts rather than the accumulation personal wealth—all within a secular framework.

It's a Wonderful Life

Life is wonderful, even without belief in any gods and the promise of eternal paradise. I consider myself extremely fortunate to continually experience such a high level of well-being, and I know that I am not alone. There are countless non-believers living good lives, but there are also many for whom religion is so deeply ingrained that they cannot conceive of flourishing in a world without adopting the myths of our ancestors. It is my hope that positive humanism provides everyone with a way to live better lives— secular lives, debunks the myths that atheists are evil or immoral people who can't be trusted, and promotes and encourages a culture of prosocial acts, which are unconstrained by superstition and "divine" limitations.

For more information about me and to see what I am currently up to, please visit BoBennett.com.

References

Caldwell-Harris, C. L., Wilson, A. L., LoTempio, E., & Beit-Hallahmi, B. (2011). Exploring the atheist personality: well-being, awe, and magical thinking in atheists, Buddhists, and Christians. *Mental Health, Religion & Culture*, *14*(7), 659–672. doi:10.1080/13674676.2010.509847

Fredrickson, B. L., & Losada, M. F. (2005). Positive affect and the complex dynamics of human flourishing. *The American Psychologist*, *60*(7), 678–686. doi:10.1037/0003-066X.60.7.678

Hanna, T. L. (1956). Albert Camus and the Christian faith. *The Journal of Religion*, *Vol. 36*(No. 4 (Oct., 1956)), pp. 224–233.

Hogg, M. A., Adelman, J. R., & Blagg, R. D. (2010). Religion in the face of uncertainty: An uncertainty-identity theory account of religiousness. *Personality and Social Psychology Review*, *14*(1), 72–83. doi:10.1177/1088868309349692

Huppert, F. A., & So, T. T. C. (2013). Flourishing across Europe: Application of a new conceptual framework for defining well-being. *Social Indicators Research*, *110*(3), 837–861. doi:10.1007/s11205-011-9966-7

Hursthouse, R. (1991). Arational actions. *The Journal of Philosophy*, *88*(2), 57–68.

Pinker, S. (1999). How the Mind Works. *Annals of the New York Academy of Sciences*, *882*(1), 119–127. doi:10.1111/j.1749-6632.1999.tb08538.x

Richards, R. J. (1989). *Darwin and the Emergence of Evolutionary Theories of Mind and Behavior*. University of Chicago Press.

Rudd, M., Aaker, J., & Norton, M. I. (2014). Getting the most out of giving: Concretely framing a prosocial goal maximizes happiness. *Journal of Experimental Social Psychology*. doi: 10.1016/j.jesp.2014.04.002

Seligman, M. E. P. (2012). *Flourish: A visionary new understanding of happiness and well-being*. Simon and Schuster.

Seul, J. R. (1999). 'Ours is the way of God': Religion, identity, and intergroup conflict. *Journal of Peace Research*, *36*(5), 553–569. doi:10.1177/0022343399036005004

Smith, P. C., Range, L. M., & Ulmer, A. (1991). Belief in afterlife as a buffer in suicidal and other bereavement. *OMEGA--Journal of Death and Dying*, *24*(3), 217–225. doi:10.2190/HME4-G1XE-9HXL-TJ96

What Alabamians and Iranians Have in Common. (n.d.). Retrieved April 27, 2014, from http://www.gallup.com/poll/114211/alabamians-iranians-common.aspx